boyzone
greatest hits so far...

This publication is not authorised for sale in the United States of America and / or Canada

Wise Publications

London / New York / Sydney / Paris / Copenhagen / Madrid

Exclusive Distributors:

Music Sales Limited
8/9 Frith Street,
London W1V 5TZ, England.

Music Sales Pty Limited
120 Rothschild Avenue
Rosebery, NSW 2018, Australia.

Order No. AM949300
ISBN 0-7119-7354-7

This book © Copyright 1999 by
Wise Publications.
www.musicinprint.com

Unauthorised reproduction of
any part of this publication by
any means including photocopying is
an infringement of copyright.

Book design by Michael Bell Design.

Printed in Great Britain by
Printwise (Haverhill) Limited, Suffolk.

Your Guarantee of Quality:

As publishers, we strive to
produce every book to
the highest commercial standards.
The book has been carefully designed to
minimise awkward page turns and to
make playing from it a real pleasure.
Particular care has been given to
specifying acid-free, neutral-sized
paper made from pulps which have not
been elemental chlorine bleached.

This pulp is from farmed sustainable forests and
was produced with special regard for the environment.
Throughout, the printing and binding have
been planned to ensure a sturdy, attractive
publication which should give years of enjoyment.
If your copy fails to meet our high standards,
please inform us and we will gladly replace it.

Music Sales' complete catalogue
describes thousands of titles and is available in
full colour sections by subject,
direct from Music Sales Limited.
Please state your areas of interest and
send a cheque/postal order for
£1.50 for postage to: Music Sales Limited,
Newmarket Road, Bury St. Edmunds, Suffolk IP33 3YB.

no matter what

Music by Andrew Lloyd Webber. Lyrics by Jim Steinman.

Unhurried

No mat - ter what they tell us, no mat - ter what they do,
If on - ly tears were laugh - ter, if on - ly night was day,

no mat - ter what they teach us, what we be - lieve is true.
if on - ly prayers were an - swered then we would hear God say.

© Copyright 1999 The Really Useful Group Limited, 22 Tower Street, London WC2 (50%) &
Lost Boys Music / PolyGram Music Publishing Limited, 47 British Grove, London W4 (50%).
All Rights Reserved. International Copyright Secured.

I know our love's for-ev-er,
No mat-ter where it's bar-ren

I know no mat-ter what.
our dream is be-ing born.

f Instrumental

No mat-ter who they fol-low, no mat-ter where they lead,

no mat-ter how they judge us I'll be eve-ry one you need.

No mat-ter if the sun don't shine,

or if the skies are blue. No mat-ter what the

a different beat

Words & Music by Martin Brannigan, Stephen Gately, Ronan Keating, Shane Lynch, Keith Duffy & Ray Hedges.

Let's not for-get this place,____ let's not ne-

glect our race,____ let u-ni-ty be-come,____

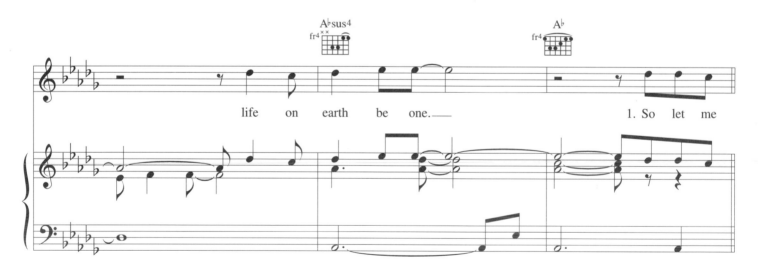

life on earth be one.____ 1. So let me

© Copyright 1996 PolyGram Music Publishing Limited, 47 British Grove, London W4 (20%),
Island Music Limited, 47 British Grove, London W4 (60%) &
19 Music/BMG Music Publishing Limited, 69-79 Fulham High Street, London SW6 (20%).
This arrangement © Copyright 1999 BMG Music Publishing Limited for their share of interest.
All Rights Reserved. International Copyright Secured.

take your hand,— we are but grains of sand,— born through the
(Verse 2 see block lyric)

winds of time,— giv-en a spe-cial sign.— So

let's take a stand and look a-round us now,— peo-ple.———— So

let's take a stand and look a-round us now,— peo-ple.———— Ee-

Verse 2:
Humanity has lost face,
Let's understand its grace,
Each day, one at a time,
Each life, including mine.

Let's take a stand and look around us now,
People,
So let's take a stand and look around us now,
People, oh people, oh people.

all that i need

Words & Music by Evan Rogers & Carl Sturken.

1. I was lost and a-lone,____ try-ing to grow,
(Verse 2 see block lyric)

____ mak-ing my way____ down that long____ wind-ing road.____ Had no rea-son or rhyme

© Copyright 1995 Bayjun Beat Music/Music Corporation of America, USA.
MCA Music Limited, 77 Fulham Palace Road, London W6.
All Rights Reserved. International Copyright Secured.

like a song out of time, and there you are stand-ing in front of my eyes. How could I be such a fool to let go of love and break all of the rules? Girl, when you walked out that door, left a hole in my heart and now I know for sure;

You're the air that I breathe_____ girl, you're all that I need._____

And I wan-na thank__ you la-dy._____ You're the words that I read,-

_____ you're the light that I see,_____ and your love is all____ that I need.__

Verse 2:
I was searching in vain, playing your game
Had no-one else but myself left to blame
You came into my world, no diamonds or pearls
Could ever replace what you gave to me girl
Just like a castle of sand
Girl I almost let love
Slip right out of my hand
And just like a flower needs rain
I will stand by your side
Through the joy and the pain.

You're the air that I breathe *etc.*

coming home now

Words & Music by Stephen Gately, Ronan Keating, Michael Graham, Shane Lynch & Keith Duffy.

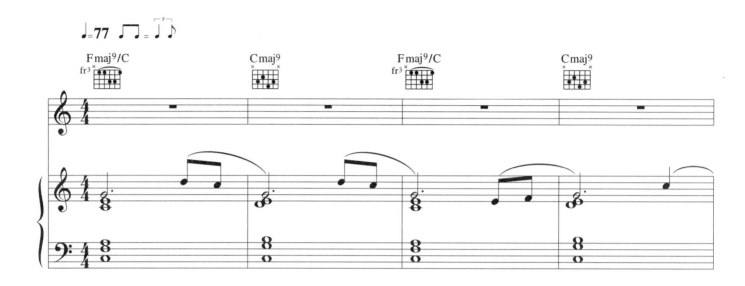

© Copyright 1995 PolyGram Music Publishing Limited, 47 British Grove, London W4 (25%),
Island Music Limited, 47 British Grove, London W4 (50%) &
19 Music/BMG Music Publishing Limited, 69-79 Fulham High Street, London SW6 (25%).
This arrangement © Copyright 1999 BMG Music Publishing Limited for their share of interest.
All Rights Reserved. International Copyright Secured.

Da da da da da da.— Da da da da da da.— A kiss on the cheek— in the old— town park,—

carved your name— in the shape of a heart,— walked to - ge - ther hand in hand,—

I did-n't feel the rain._____ And there's a

pic - ture, girl,_____ that hangs in - side my mind,_____ and there's a let - ter, girl,— say I'm do - ing

now, _____ it's been so long ___ now. _____ Gon-na get there some-

- how, _____ pray-ing you'll be there. Weeks, days till I'll be there.

Child-ren on the streets still play-ing their games, the smiles on their fa-ces have ne-ver changed. ___

I hope it's all the same, _____

D.%. al Coda

I did-n't leave in vain. And there's a

Coda

now, it's been so long now. Gon-na get there some-

how, and this is where I'll stay, and this is where I'll

stay.

Spoken: "Dearly close words: I really want to see you. You're in my heart when overseas. I feel you close, and not so far. Soon we'll be together, and this time it's forever.

I'm

ben

Words by Don Black. Music by Walter Scharf.

1. Ben, the two of us need look no more, we both found what we were
(Verses 2 & 3 see block lyric)

look-ing for. With a friend to call my own, I'll nev-er be a-

© Copyright 1971, 1972 Jobete Music Company Incorporated, USA.
Jobete Music (UK) Limited, London WC2 for the UK and Eire.
All Rights Reserved. International Copyright Secured.

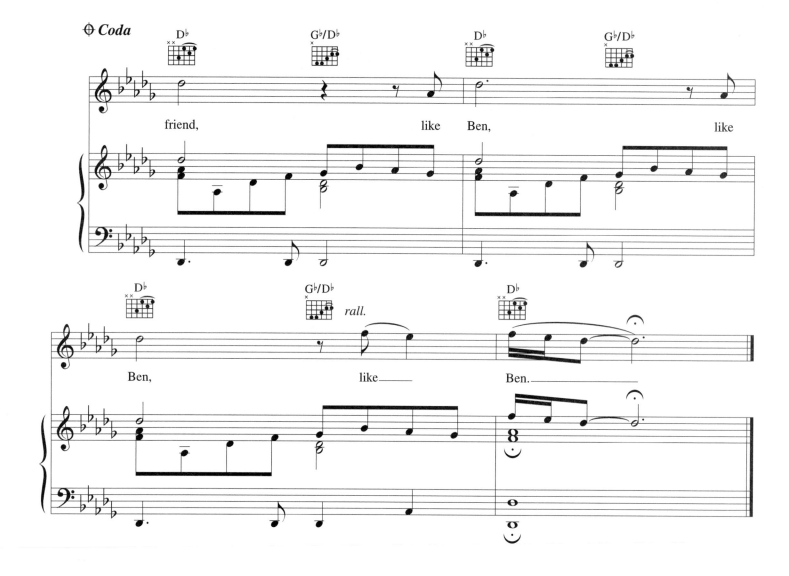

Verse 2:

Ben, you're always running here and there,
You feel you're not wanted anywhere.
If you ever look behind
And don't like what you find,
There's one thing you should know:
You've got a place to go.

Verse 3:

Ben, most people would turn you away,
I don't listen to a word they say.
They don't see you as I do,
I wish they would try to;
I'm sure they'd think again
If they had a friend like Ben.

father and son

Words & Music by Cat Stevens.

time to make a change; just re-lax, take it ea-sy. You're still
(Verse 2 see block lyric)

young, that's your fault; there's so much you have to know. Find a girl,

© Copyright 1970 Cat Music Limited.
All Rights Reserved. International Copyright Secured.

set-tle down;— if you want,— you— can mar - ry. Look at me:—

1. I am old— but I'm hap - py. 2. I was

2. be here— to - mor - row,— but your dreams may not.

How can I— try to ex - plain?— When I do—
(Verse 4 see block lyric)

28

go.   3. It's not

time   to make a   change,—   just   sit   down—   and take it   slow - ly. You're still

young,   that's your   fault;—   there's so   much   you   have— to   go through. Find— a   girl,—

— set - tle   down;—   if you   want,—   you— can mar - ry. Look at me—

Verse 2:

I was once like you are now;
And I know that it's not easy
To be calm when you've found something going on.
But take your time, think a lot;
Think of everything you've got.
For you will still be here tomorrow,
But your dreams may not.

Verse 4:

All the times that I've cried,
Keeping all the things I knew inside;
And it's hard, but it's harder to ignore it.
If they were right I'd agree,
But it's them they know, not me;
Now there's a way, and I know
That I have to go away.
I know I have to go.

i love the way you love me

Words & Music by Chuck Cannon & Victoria Shaw.

1. I like the feel__ of your name on my lips and I like the sound__ of your sweet

© Copyright 1993 Wacissa River Music, USA.
BMG Music Publishing Limited, Bedford House, 69-79 Fulham High Street, London SW6 (37.5%) & Copyright Control (62.5%).
This arrangement © Copyright 1999 BMG Music Publishing Limited for their share of interest.
All Rights Reserved. International Copyright Secured.

gen - tle___ kiss,___ the way that your fin - gers run___ through my___ hair___ and

how your scent lin - gers ev - en when you're___ not___ there.___ 2. And

I like the way___ your eyes dance when you laugh and how you'll en - joy___ your two___
(Verse 3 see block lyrics)

___ hour___ bath___ and how you con - vinced___ me to dance in the rain___ with

Verse 3:
And I like the sound of old R and B
You roll your eyes when I'm slightly off key
And I like the innocent way that you cry
From sappy old movies you've seen thousands of times.

But I love *etc.*

key to my life

Words & Music by Martin Brannigan, Stephen Gately, Ronan Keating, Michael Graham & Ray Hedges.

© Copyright 1995 PolyGram Music Publishing Limited, 47 British Grove, London W4 (25%),
Island Music Limited, 47 British Grove, London W4 (50%) &
19 Music/BMG Music Publishing Limited, 69-79 Fulham High Street, London SW6 (25%).
This arrangement © Copyright 1999 BMG Music Publishing Limited for their share of interest.
All Rights Reserved. International Copyright Secured.

locked up in-side,___ but you came a-long___ and cap-tured my heart___ girl,

To Coda ⊕ |1.

you're the key___ to my life.

|2.

life.
Girl you know___ that I feel for you, there ain't no-thing that I would-n't do,

stop the thun-der and the pour-ing rain, you're the one___ that's gon-na stop the pain.

Verse 2:
Year after year was blaming myself
For what I'd done just thought of myself
I know that you'll understand this was all my fault
Don't go away.

love me for a reason

Words & Music by John Bristol, Wade Brown Jr & David Jones Jr.

1. Girl, when you hold_____ me,
(Verses 2 & 3 see block lyric)

how you con - trol__ me; you bend   and you fold__ me   an - y way you please.__

© Copyright 1972 Jobete Music Company Incorporated, USA.
Jobete Music (UK) Limited, London WC2 for the UK and Eire.
All Rights Reserved. International Copyright Secured.

let the rea - son be love.

D.%. al Coda

Coda

Don't love me for fun,— girl, let me be— the one, girl, love me for a rea - son,

let the rea - son be love. Don't love me for fun,— girl, let me be— the one, girl;

Verse 2:
Kisses and caresses are only minor tests, babe,
Of love needs and stresses between a woman and a man.
So if love everlasting isn't what you're asking,
I'll have to pass, girl; I'm proud to take a stand.
I can't continue guessing, because it's only messing
With my pride and my mind.
So write down this time to time:

To Chorus

Verse 3:
I'm just a little old-fashioned,
It takes more than a physical attraction.
My initial reaction is "Honey, give me love;
Not a facsimile of."

To Chorus

picture of you

Words & Music by Eliot Kennedy, Ronan Keating, Paul Wilson & Andy Watkins.

Did-n't I say that I would make a mis-take?__ Did-n't they say you were gon-na be trou-ble?__ Lay parts on me who were too much to take, I could-n't see

© Copyright 1997 Island Music Limited, 47 British Grove, London W4 (10%),
Sony/ATV Music Publishing, 10 Great Marlborough Street, London W1 (25%) &
19 Music Limited/BMG Music Publishing Limited, Bedford House, 69-79 Fulham High Street, London SW6 (65%).
This arrangement © Copyright 1999 BMG Music Publishing Limited for their share of interest.
All Rights Reserved. International Copyright Secured.

Verse 2:
Do you believe that after all that we've been through
I'd be able to put my trust in you?
Goes to show you can forgive and forget
Looking back I have no regrets, cos

You were with me there *etc.*

when all is said and done

Words & Music by Martin Brannigan, Stephen Gately, Ronan Keating, Michael Graham, Shane Lynch, Keith Duffy & Ray Hedges.

1. Days that we spent — when I was so small, —
(Verse 2 see block lyric)

ne - ver let me fall, — you ne - ver let me fall.

© Copyright 1995 PolyGram Music Publishing Limited, 47 British Grove, London W4 (45%),
Island Music Limited, 47 British Grove, London W4 (10%) &
19 Music/BMG Music Publishing Limited, 69-79 Fulham High Street, London SW6 (25%).
This arrangement © Copyright 1999 BMG Music Publishing Limited for their share of interest.
All Rights Reserved. International Copyright Secured.

Taught me to see___ the right and the wrong;___ oh, I'm not that strong,___ wish I was that strong.___ You've been good___ to me, tend-ing my ev-'ry need. Just look___ what I am,___

Verse 2:
Now I'm a man, time has gone fast;
I didn't want it to, I didn't want it to.
Went on my way like a crazy young fool;
I never wanted to, I never wanted to.
You've been good *etc.*

words

Words & Music by Barry Gibb, Robin Gibb & Maurice Gibb.

Moderately slow

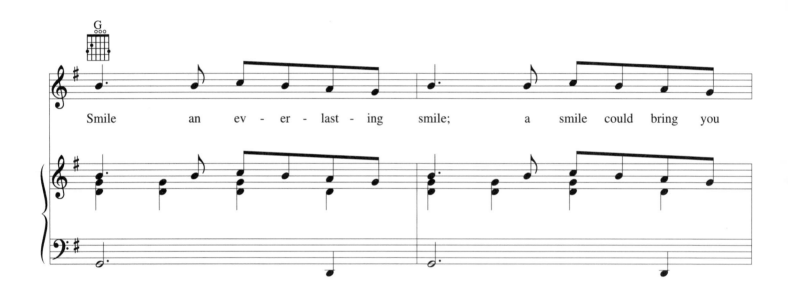

Smile an ev - er - last - ing smile; a smile could bring you

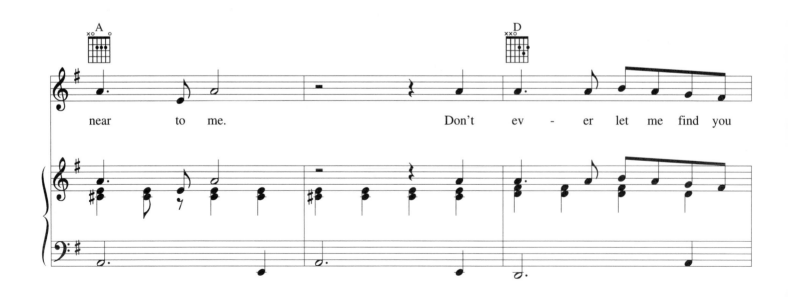

near to me. Don't ev - er let me find you

© Copyright 1967 & 1975 Gibb Brothers Music.
All Rights Reserved. International Copyright Secured.

Talk in ev-er-last-ing words and ded-i-cate them all to me.

And I will give you all my life, I'm here if you should

call to me. You think that I don't e-ven

mean a sin-gle word I say. It's on-ly

so good

Words & Music by Martin Brannigan, Stephen Gately, Ronan Keating, Michael Graham, Shane Lynch, Keith Duffy & Ray Hedges.

© Copyright 1995 PolyGram Music Publishing Limited, 47 British Grove, London W4 (25%),
Island Music Limited, 47 British Grove, London W4 (50%) &
19 Music / BMG Music Publishing Limited, 69-79 Fulham High Street, London SW6 (25%).
This arrangement © Copyright 1999 BMG Music Publishing Limited for their share of interest.
All Rights Reserved. International Copyright Secured.

Coda ⊕

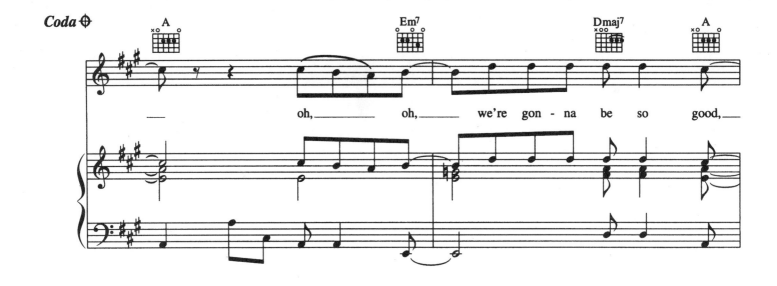

oh,_____ oh,_____ we're gon - na be so good,_____

_____ like I knew we would,_____ you know we're good._____

Verse 2:
No matter the cost
When we're out on the town getting lazy
I'll show you who's boss
We're just gonna take it all the way
No matter what they say now.

7/99 (34575)